Rules Rap

The rules, the rules, the rules of the classroom.
The rules, the rules, the rules of the classroom.

Follow, follow, follow directions.
Follow, follow, follow directions.

The rules, the rules, the rules of the classroom.
The rules, the rules, the rules of the classroom.

Feet and hands, feet and hands,
feet and hands to yourself.
Feet and hands, feet and hands,
feet and hands to yourself.

The rules, the rules, the rules of the classroom.
The rules, the rules, the rules of the classroom.

Small voices inside,
tall voices on the playground.
Small voices inside,
tall voices on the playground.

The rules, the rules, the rules of the classroom.
The rules, the rules, the rules of the classroom.

Take care of your things,
and keep the classroom neat and clean.
Take care of your things,
and keep the classroom neat and clean.

The rules, the rules, the rules of the classroom.
The rules, the rules, the rules of the classroom.

Work together, get along, and respect each other.
Work together, get along, and respect each other.

The rules, the rules, the rules of the classroom.
The rules, the rules, the rules of the classroom.

The rules, the rules, the rules of the classroom.
The rules, the rules, the rules of the classroom.
YEAH!